Mug Cakes

Mug Cakes

40 SPEEDY CAKES TO MAKE IN A MICROWAVE

MIMA SINCLAIR

KYLE BOOKS

To my mother, who has never hidden her love of sugar,
and to my dad, who said I would grow out of mine.

First published in 2014 by
Kyle Books
www.kylebooks.com general.
enquiries@kylebooks.com

Distributed by National Book
Network
4501 Forbes Blvd., Suite 200
Lanham, MD 20706
Phone: (800) 462-6420
Fax: (800) 338-4550
customercare@nbnbooks.com

10 9 8 7 6 5 4 3 2 1

ISBN 978-1-909487-19-2

Editor: Judith Hannam
Project editor: Vicki Murrell
Designer: Nicola Collings
Photographer: Tara Fisher
Food stylist: Mima Sinclair
Prop stylists: Wei Tang, Olivia
Wardle
Illustrations: Aaron Blecha
Production: Nic Jones, Gemma John

Library of Congress Control No.
2014942805

Color reproduction by ALTA
London
Printed and bound in Singapore by
Tien Wah Press

CONTENTS

WHAT IS A MUG CAKE?

Make a cake in a mug, in a microwave, in less than 10 minutes, using simple ingredients, with no waste, no leftovers, and little washing up? Where's the catch? There isn't one.

Conventional cake making can be tricky, as we've all learned through trial and error. There is such an exact science behind it that a little too much of this, or not enough of that, can have dramatic consequences—both costly and time-consuming. On the other hand, mug cakes—instant cakes you make in the microwave using simple measurements and minimal ingredients—make baking so easy you will soon be creating your own recipes.

I experimented a lot with different approaches and quantities of ingredients, initially with mixed results. The main differences between an oven and a microwave are the way they heat food and the speed at which they do it. This affects two things—the microwave can't brown or crisp a cake, and just as it cooks the cake faster, it also dries it out faster if you overcook it. There were some explosions and a fair bit of mess, but as soon as I learned a few do's and don'ts, I was creating perfect cakes time and time again. Once I'd mastered a deliciously light cake, it was exciting seeing what flavors I could mix in and complement with fun frostings and toppings. I'm a bit of a sugar addict, so for me it's all about the toppings! The possibilities are endless, and that's what is really exciting—not only can you make cake in the microwave, you can make cheesecakes, upside down cakes, happy hour cocktails, cookies, and more! They are perfect single-serving cakes to save you munching a whole baked one! They're also great for hungry kids, who'll think it's an extra treat to be able to make the cake themselves. And as dinner party desserts and unique party nibbles that will surely get people talking.

Mug cakes are fun, quick fixes that you'll enjoy as soon as you decide you want one. The only problem is that when they are this easy, every night becomes a mug cake night!

THE INGREDIENTS

BUTTER

In testing, I found that soft, room temperature butter was best for ensuring cakes have a delicious, rich flavor, but you can also use a flavorless oil (such as sunflower or vegetable), or even margarine. Just swap in the recipe in place of the butter, because the measurements are like for like. If you use butter straight from the refrigerator it will just take a little longer to melt.

EGGS

Always use large eggs because other sizes will upset the balance of ingredients in the cake mix. I find they are best when used at room temperature; otherwise they can curdle easily and cause the mixture to separate. However, if this happens, it really is not a problem—the cake will just be a little less light.

SALT

This can be omitted if you wish, but using salt as a seasoning really enhances the overall flavor of both sweet and savory cakes and intensifies them.

SUGAR

The recipes mainly call for superfine or brown sugar because these have a finer texture than granulated and other, coarser sugars, so are better for baking because they dissolve quicker when cooking. You can make your own superfine sugar by briefly grinding granulated sugar in a food processor (although be careful you don't overgrind to a powder).

FLOUR

These recipes all call for a combination of all-purpose flour plus some baking powder as a rising agent. But self-rising flour is also convenient to use since the balance of flour and baking powder has been measured out for you. If you happen to have some in the house, swap it in for the all-purpose flour, but omit the baking powder. Nice and simple!

READY... SET...

You need no special kitchen utensils or culinary baking skills—just a mug, a microwave, and a few basic ingredients, so you're probably ready to go! However, as microwaves and explosions do occasionally go hand in hand, read here to avoid any mishaps and guarantee instant mug cake success.

THE MUG

Is it microwavable? This is important. If it isn't, the high heat of a microwave may cause it to crack and scald you. Check for a microwave symbol, and if you can't see one, perform the quick test on the right.

THE MICROWAVE

What type? Microwave ovens, like conventional ovens, do vary in power and age, which effects the cooking times so they are inevitably a little approximate. You may need to use your judgment to decide if it needs a little more or less cooking time. However, I have created these recipes using a standard microwave that will no doubt be very similar to what you have in your kitchen, and I always include three standard microwave power wattages so you have a few options. Use the closest to that of your microwave, follow the timings as a guideline, and bear in mind the Essential Do's and Don'ts that follow, and you will quickly get the hang of it.

THE MUG TEST

Place the (empty) mug in the microwave and heat for 1 minute. Take it out and feel its temperature. If it's lukewarm or cold then it should be fine, but if it's hot, do not use it in your microwave.

Is it metal? Do not use metal mugs or anything with a metallic trim such as a gold band or pattern. They can produce dangerous sparks that could burn you or damage the microwave.

Size counts. The average size of a mug is 1½ cups. Check out your favorite mug before you use it—if it is larger, it is not a problem, but if it is smaller you will need to leave a little of the mixture out to avoid a messy overflow. If you want to get inventive and start serving cakes in containers other than mugs, such as ramekins, jars, ice cream cones, cardboard cups, etc, just bear in mind the size difference (they are often smaller) and don't overfill them. Or make two—one for you and a friend. Just remember to avoid anything metal, even if it's just a tiny trimming.

Do not be disheartened if your cake sinks or explodes. The finished product will still taste delicious. You will soon work out the timings and quantities for your microwave.

Do not be tempted to keep cooking the cake until it browns or forms a crust—it never will! Unlike conventional ovens, microwaves do not directly brown or caramelize food because they don't reach the necessary temperatures. If you continue to cook a mug cake, it will just dry out.

THE ESSENTIAL DO'S AND DON'TS

(OR HOW TO AVOID AN AWFUL MESS)

PREP

Do not overwhisk because this overaerates the cake batter and, once cooked, you may discover air holes in the cake (not ideal if your cake is in any kind of glass container).

Do not underwhisk either because this will also result in air pockets due to a mass of unmixed butter or flour. Whisk the ingredients together with a fork until the cake batter is smooth.

Do not overfill the mug. Two-thirds full is plenty or the batter is likely to spill, lava-like, right over the edges.

Line the mug with plastic wrap if you are planning on turning it out. Alternatively, grease it with a little oil or butter.

COOKING

Place a plate under the mug. This will minimize the clean-up if there is an unexpected overflow or explosion!

Be patient. Wait for at least three-quarters of the cooking time before you check on your cake or it will sink. Don't worry if it does—it will rise again, just follow the directions below.

Is it done? If the cake rapidly sinks once you open the microwave door, the cake is not cooked through. Return it to the microwave and cook in bursts of 15 seconds until risen and it no longer sinks.

It looks done. If your cake is perfectly risen, touch the top of the cake in the center—it should feel firm and slightly springy. You can also try the classic cake test; insert a skewer right down to the base of the mug and check to see, when you remove it, that it comes out clean. Alternatively, use a knife to pull the cake away from the edge to see to all the way to the bottom of the mug. If it is still a little uncooked, return it to the microwave and cook for short bursts of time, making sure not to overcook it.

It's a little underdone. This could be exactly what you're after if you like a slightly gooey center.

DECORATING

Cool the cake properly before frosting to prevent it melting. This could be your desired effect, but not when you go to the effort of beautifully piping your friend's name and it dribbles all over the place.

If you are turning the cake out onto a plate, the cake should come out cleanly as long as you remembered to grease the mug or line it with plastic wrap. If you forgot this step, run a small knife or offset spatula between the cake and the mug and ease it out carefully.

ENJOY

Eat right away! Mug cakes are best eaten on the day they are made since they dry out more quickly than conventionally baked cakes. If you do want to keep it until the next day, either cover with icing to seal in the moisture or wrap well with foil.

GO!

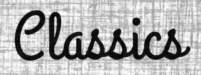

CHOCOLATE & PEANUT BUTTER

*If you had to work late, your train was delayed, or you got caught in the rain...
this is the cake to treat yourself with—it will chase your blues away.*

INGREDIENTS

2 tablespoons butter, softened

1½ ounces dark chocolate, finely
chopped

1 large egg

2 tablespoons 2% milk

3 tablespoons superfine sugar

3 tablespoons all-purpose flour

¼ teaspoon baking powder

pinch of salt

2 tablespoons smooth peanut butter

1 tablespoon salted roasted peanuts,
roughly chopped

METHOD

Place the butter and chocolate in a 1½ cup mug and
microwave for 10–20 seconds until melted.

Add the egg and milk to the mug and beat with a fork until
thoroughly combined.

Add the sugar, flour, baking powder, and salt, and beat again
until smooth, then float a tablespoon of peanut butter on top
of the cake mixture but don't stir—this will sink down as the
cake cooks to create a lovely gooey peanut butter center.

Cook in the microwave for 2 minutes 20 seconds @ 600W,
2 minutes @ 800W, or 1 minute 40 seconds @ 1000W.

While the cake is still warm, top with the remaining peanut
butter. Wait for it to melt slightly and then sprinkle with
peanuts, curl up on the sofa, and enjoy.

Swap

Overdose on chocolate—
swap the peanut butter
for chocolate spread.

CARROT CAKE

Carrot cake as it should be, with pecans, raisins, and a delicious cream cheese topping.

INGREDIENTS

2 tablespoons vegetable oil

1 large egg

1 tablespoon 2% milk

1 teaspoon vanilla extract

3 tablespoons light brown sugar

4 tablespoons flour

¼ teaspoon baking powder

pinch of salt

¼ teaspoon pumpkin pie spice

¼ teaspoon cinnamon

2 tablespoons grated carrot

½ tablespoon pecans, roughly
  chopped

½ tablespoon raisins

To decorate

2 tablespoons cream cheese

1 tablespoon confectioner's sugar

1 teaspoon lemon juice

¼ teaspoon cinnamon

1–2 edible sugar carrots

METHOD

Place the oil, egg, milk, vanilla, and sugar in a 1½ cup mug and beat with a fork until well combined.

Add the flour, baking powder, salt, pumpkin pie spice, and cinnamon, and beat again until smooth, then fold in the carrot, pecans and raisins.

Cook in the microwave for 2 minutes 35 seconds @ 600W, 2 minutes 15 minutes @ 800W, or 1 minute 55 seconds @ 1000W. Leave to cool.

Meanwhile, make the frosting. Beat together the cream cheese, confectioner's sugar, and lemon juice until light and fluffy.

Roughly spoon the frosting over the cooled cake. Sprinkle on the cinnamon and top with a sugar carrot or two.

Tip

You can easily make your own carrot toppers with a little marzipan and food coloring.

VANILLA CONES

The perfect treat for a sunny afternoon! Kids love them, so why not start a trend and serve them at parties instead of cupcakes?

INGREDIENTS

2 tablespoons butter, softened

1 large egg

1 tablespoon 2% milk

2 teaspoons vanilla extract

3 tablespoons superfine sugar

4 tablespoons all-purpose flour

¼ teaspoon baking powder

pinch of salt

4 small flat-bottomed wafer ice
  cream cones, optional

To decorate

4 tablespoons butter, softened

6 tablespoons confectioner's sugar

¼ teaspoon vanilla extract

1 tablespoon strawberry sauce

1 teaspoon colored sprinkles

2 chocolate flakes, halved

Tip

Alter the frosting flavor
by adding 1 tablespoon
cooled melted chocolate
or jam or 1 teaspoon
flavored essence.

METHOD

Place the butter in a mug and microwave for 10–20 seconds until melted.

Add the egg, milk, and vanilla to the mug and beat together with a fork. Add the sugar, flour, baking powder, and salt, and beat again until smooth.

Divide among the four ice cream cones and place on a small plate. Cook in the microwave for 1 minute 45 seconds @ 600W, 1 minute 30 seconds @ 800W, or 1 minute 15 seconds @ 1000W. Leave to cool.

Meanwhile, make the frosting. Beat the butter, confectioner's sugar, and vanilla together until light and fluffy, then spoon into a piping bag fitted with a large open star nozzle.

Pipe the frosting over the cooled cake in a spiral pattern—it's best to work from the outside edge, keeping a constant pressure on the piping bag as you work in toward the center. To finish, release the pressure on the bag, then press down lightly and pull straight up. Decorate with all the sauces and sprinkles that take your fancy.

If using a 1½ cup mug instead of the cones, cook in the microwave for 2 minutes 50 seconds @ 600W, 2 minutes 30 seconds @ 800W, or 2 minutes 10 seconds @ 1000W. Leave to cool. To make the icing, use half the butter, confectioner's sugar, and vanilla.

TRIPLE CHOCOLATE CAKE

So decadent but so good! I can't imagine life without chocolate cake, so go on, treat yourself.

INGREDIENTS

2 tablespoons butter, softened
1½ ounces dark chocolate, finely
   chopped
1 large egg
2 tablespoons 2% milk
3 tablespoons superfine sugar
3 tablespoons all-purpose flour
¼ teaspoon baking powder
pinch of salt

Chocolate ganache
6 tablespoons heavy cream
2 ounces dark chocolate, finely
   chopped

The longer you leave the ganache, the more it will set, so keep an eye on it.

METHOD

First make the chocolate ganache. Place 4 tablespoons of the heavy cream in a mug and microwave for 30 seconds until nearly boiling. Add the finely chopped chocolate and mix until melted and smooth, then set aside to cool and thicken.

Grease a 1½ cup mug with a little butter and set aside. Place the remaining butter and chocolate in a second mug and microwave for 10–20 seconds until melted.

Add the egg and milk to the mug and beat with a fork until thoroughly combined. Add the sugar, flour, baking powder, and salt and beat again until smooth.

Pour the cake mixture into the greased mug and cook in the microwave for 2 minutes 20 seconds @ 600W, 2 minutes @ 800W, or 1 minute 40 seconds @ 1000W. Leave to cool slightly because the cake will shrink a little from the sides of the mug.

Turn the cake out onto a plate and pour on the ganache to serve. Whip the remaining cream into soft peaks and spoon a flourish on top.

CHOCOLATE BROWNIE

Make a brownie in a small paper cup or ice cream container, and you can slip one into a lunchbox or pack a bunch for a picnic.

INGREDIENTS

2 tablespoons butter, softened

2 tablespoons superfine sugar

1 tablespoon brown sugar

1 tablespoon cocoa powder

1 large egg yolk

½ teaspoon vanilla extract

4 tablespoons all-purpose flour

¼ teaspoon baking powder

pinch of salt

2 tablespoons chocolate chips

METHOD

Place the butter in a 1 cup teacup or small mug and microwave for 10–20 seconds until melted.

Add the superfine sugar, brown sugar, and cocoa powder, and beat with a fork until thoroughly combined.

Add the egg yolk and vanilla and beat together, then add the flour, baking powder, and salt and beat again until thoroughly combined and smooth. Stir in half the chocolate chips and transfer to a paper cup, if using.

Cook in the microwave for 50 seconds @ 600W, 30 seconds @ 800W, or 25 seconds @ 1000W. Scatter the remaining chocolate chips over the top and cook in the microwave for another 30 seconds. Leave to cool—I recommend about 15 minutes (if you can bear to wait) so the cake becomes deliciously chewy and is ready to serve.

Tip Try under-cooking this brownie just a little for a gooey center… yum!

BANANA BREAD

Moist, sticky, and sweet… just the way banana bread should be.

INGREDIENTS

1 medium ripe banana

1 tablespoon vegetable oil

1 large egg

1 tablespoon 2% milk

4 tablespoons brown sugar

4 tablespoons all-purpose flour

¼ teaspoon baking powder

pinch of salt

¼ teaspoon cinnamon

1 tablespoon pecans, roughly
  chopped

1 tablespoon golden raisins

To decorate

2 tablespoons cream cheese

1 tablespoon confectioner's sugar

1 teaspoon lemon juice

¼ teaspoon cinnamon

METHOD

In a 1½ cup mug, mash ¾ of the banana (reserving the rest) with a fork, and then beat in the oil, egg, and milk until well combined.

Add the sugar, flour, baking powder, salt, and cinnamon, and beat again until smooth. Fold in the pecans and golden raisins.

Cook in the microwave for 3 minutes 20 seconds @ 600W, 3 minutes @ 800W, or 2 minutes 40 seconds @ 1000W. Leave to cool.

Meanwhile, make the frosting. Place the cream cheese, confectioner's sugar and lemon juice in a medium bowl and beat with a fork or a whisk until light and fluffy. Slice the remaining ¼ banana. Spoon the frosting into a piping bag fitted with a closed star nozzle. Pipe at a 45° angle, then top with slices of banana and the cinnamon. Serve immediately.

Tip Perfect for the sad looking black banana in your fruit bowl.

COFFEE & WALNUT CAKE

This is an old classic that never goes out of style and in my opinion is the perfect cake for a midmorning snack or afternoon tea... especially when it comes with a creamy caramel topping!

INGREDIENTS

2 tablespoons butter, softened

2 teaspoons instant coffee mixed with 1 tablespoon hot water

1 large egg

1 teaspoon vanilla extract

3 tablespoons superfine sugar

4 tablespoons all-purpose flour

¼ teaspoon baking powder

pinch of salt

1 tablespoon walnuts, roughly chopped

To decorate

2 tablespoons heavy cream

½ tablespoon caramel sauce

1 walnut half

METHOD

Place the butter in a 1½ cup mug and microwave for 10–20 seconds until melted.

Add the coffee, egg, vanilla, and sugar to the mug and beat with a fork until thoroughly combined. Add the flour, baking powder, and salt and beat again until smooth, then fold in the walnut pieces. Cook in the microwave for 2 minutes @ 600W, 1 minute 45 seconds @ 800W or 1 minute 30 seconds @ 1000W. Leave to cool.

Meanwhile, make the frosting. Whip the cream into soft peaks, fold in the caramel sauce, and then spoon over the cooled cake and top with the walnut half.

Tip For a little extra luxury, replace the cream in the frosting with mascarpone.

BLUEBERRY MUFFIN

This is so delicious and so easy…
just don't get into the habit of eating one for breakfast every day!

INGREDIENTS

2 tablespoons butter, softened

1 large egg

1 tablespoon 2% milk

1 teaspoon vanilla extract

3 tablespoons brown sugar

4 tablespoons all-purpose flour

¼ teaspoon baking powder

¼ teaspoon cinnamon

pinch of salt

3 tablespoons fresh blueberries

½ teaspoon brown sugar for
   sprinkling

METHOD

Place the butter in a 1½ cup mug and microwave for 10–20 seconds until melted.

Add the egg, milk, and vanilla to the mug and beat with a fork until thoroughly combined.

Add the sugar, flour, baking powder, cinnamon, and salt, and beat again until smooth. Fold in half the blueberries and then top with the remainder.

Cook in the microwave for 2 minutes 20 seconds @ 600W, 2 minutes @ 800W, or 1 minute 40 seconds @ 1000W.

Sprinkle with the brown sugar and serve while it is still a little warm.

Swap raspberries for the blueberries or little chunks of pear—and if you do that, throw in a few chocolate chips, too, since they go so well together!

GLUTEN-FREE CHOCOLATE CAKE

Gluten-free flour is widely available and can be used to make very successful mug cakes ... so you can have your cake and eat it, too!

INGREDIENTS

2 tablespoons butter, softened

1½ ounces dark chocolate, finely chopped

1 large egg

2 tablespoons 2% milk

3 tablespoons superfine sugar

3 tablespoons gluten-free flour

¼ teaspoon baking powder

pinch of salt

METHOD

Place the butter and chocolate in a 1½ cup mug and microwave for 10–20 seconds until melted.

Add the egg and milk to the mug and beat with a fork until thoroughly combined. Add the sugar, flour, baking powder, and salt, and beat again until smooth.

Cook in the microwave for 2 minutes 20 seconds @ 600W, 2 minutes @ 800W or 1 minute 40 seconds @ 1000W. Leave to cool slightly and serve.

Tip

Feel free to mix and match this cake with any of the toppings from the book!

EGGLESS CHOCOLATE CAKE

Just because you can't eat eggs doesn't mean you can't join in on all the mug cake fun. This eggless cake is just as light, cakey, and delicious as its eggy companion.

INGREDIENTS

2 tablespoons butter, softened

1 tablespoon cocoa powder

2 tablespoons 2% milk

1 teaspoon vanilla extract

3 tablespoons brown sugar

4 tablespoons all-purpose flour

$\frac{1}{4}$ teaspoon baking powder

pinch of salt

2 tablespoons chocolate chips

METHOD

Place the butter in a $1\frac{1}{2}$ cup mug and microwave for 10–20 seconds until melted.

Add the cocoa powder and beat with a fork until combined. Add the milk, vanilla, and sugar to the mug and beat again until smooth.

Add the flour, baking powder, salt, and half the chocolate chips, and stir until combined. Scatter the remaining chocolate chips on top.

Cook in the microwave for 1 minute 45 seconds @ 600W, 1 minute 30 seconds @ 800W or 1 minute 15 seconds @ 1000W. Leave to cool.

Tip

Alter the flavor by using other extracts and pick a delicious topping from any of the other mug cakes.

Occasions

BLACK FOREST CAKE

*Warm, gooey chocolate cake, sweet sticky jam, fresh whipped cream,
rich chocolate curls, and a cherry on top... who could want more?*

INGREDIENTS

2 tablespoons butter, softened

1½ ounces dark chocolate, broken
into small pieces

1 large egg, lightly beaten

2 tablespoons 2% milk

3 tablespoons superfine sugar

3 tablespoons all-purpose flour

¼ teaspoon baking powder

pinch of salt

1 tablespoon cherry preserves

To decorate

¼ cup heavy cream

1 tablespoon cherry preserves

dark chocolate for garnish

fresh cherry to garnish

You can serve this cake
warm – just watch out for
dribbling cream!

METHOD

Place the butter and chocolate in a 1½ cup mug and
microwave for 10–20 seconds until melted.

Add the egg and milk to the mug and beat with a fork until
combined.

Add the sugar, flour, baking powder, and salt, and beat again
until smooth, then fold in the cherry preserves.

Cook for 2 minutes @ 600W, 1 minute 45 seconds @ 800W, or
1 minute 30 seconds @ 1000W. Leave to cool.

Meanwhile, make the frosting. Lightly whip the cream into
soft peaks. Spread the preserves over the cooled cake and then
spoon on the whipped cream. Using a vegetable peeler, create
delicate chocolate curls and scatter these over the cream.

Finish, if you like, with a cherry on top and serve immediately.

BIRTHDAY BONANZA

This makes the perfect ready-in-minutes birthday present, plus who would guess it was made in a mug when you dress it up with such fancy frosting!

INGREDIENTS

2 tablespoons butter, softened

1 large egg

1 tablespoon 2% milk

2 teaspoons vanilla extract

3 tablespoons superfine sugar

4 tablespoons flour

1/4 teaspoon baking powder

pinch of salt

1 tablespoon colored sprinkles

To decorate

1 teaspoon confectioner's sugar

Pink ready-roll fondant icing

1 tablespoon raspberry jam

3 tablespoons white icing

1 teaspoon colored sprinkles

METHOD

Place the butter in a mug and microwave for 10–20 seconds until melted.

Add the egg, milk, and vanilla to the mug and beat with a fork until combined. Add the sugar, flour, baking powder, and salt, and beat again until smooth.

Grease or line a 1 1/2 cup mug with plastic wrap, then pour in the cake batter and fold in the colored sprinkles.

Cook in the microwave for 2 minutes @ 600W, 1 minute 45 seconds @ 800W or 1 minute 30 seconds @ 1000W. Turn the cake out onto a plate, remove the plastic wrap, and leave to cool.

Meanwhile, prepare the icing. Dust the work surface with the confectioner's sugar and then roll out the pink icing to a size large enough to cover the entire cake. Spread the jam over the cake and then lay on the icing, smoothing it down with the palm of your hand as you go and trimming off any excess around the bottom with a sharp knife.

Mix the white icing with 1/2 teaspoon water to make an icing the consistency of heavy cream. Spoon this icing over the center of the cake, allowing it to trickle down the sides before it sets. Decorate with colored sprinkles.

Try this with chocolate cake (page 50) instead.

STRAWBERRIES & CREAM CAKE

*This one is a classic treat and is really a little too pretty to eat...
but I imagine you will find a way!*

INGREDIENTS

1 tablespoon butter, softened
1 large egg
1 tablespoon 2% milk
1 teaspoon vanilla extract
1½ tablespoons superfine sugar
2 tablespoons all-purpose flour
⅛ teaspoon baking powder
pinch of salt

To decorate

¼ cup heavy cream
1 tablespoon confectioner's sugar
1 tablespoon strawberry jam
1 strawberry, sliced

Tip

Stir a little elderflower
liqueur though the cream
and top with raspberries
for another unbeatable
combo.

METHOD

Place the butter in a ⅔ cup teacup and microwave for
10–20 seconds until melted.

Add the egg, milk, and vanilla to the teacup, and beat in with a
fork until combined. Add the sugar, flour, baking powder, and
salt and beat again until smooth.

Cook in the microwave for 1 minute 25 seconds @ 600W,
1 minute 15 seconds @ 800W, or 1 minute 5 seconds @
1000W. Leave to cool.

Meanwhile, make the frosting. Using a whisk or a fork, whip
the cream and confectioner's sugar into soft peaks.

Spoon the jam over the cake, then add a spoonful of cream.
Top with the strawberry and serve with a pot of Earl Grey tea.

ALMOND & BERRY BREAKFAST MUG

Earn yourself a few brownie points by treating your other half to breakfast in bed with this nut and fruit sensation.

INGREDIENTS

2 tablespoons butter, softened

1 large egg

1 tablespoon honey

3 tablespoons superfine sugar

3 tablespoons almond flour

½ teaspoon cinnamon

3 tablespoons all-purpose flour

¼ teaspoon baking powder

pinch of salt

3 tablespoons mixed berries
(eg blueberries, raspberries &
blackberries)

Streusel topping

2 teaspoons cold butter, finely
chopped

½ tablespoon all-purpose flour

pinch of baking powder

½ tablespoon superfine sugar

1 teaspoon rolled oats

pinch of cinnamon

½ tablespoon almonds, roughly
chopped

METHOD

Place the butter in a 1½ cup mug and microwave for 10–20 seconds until melted.

Add the egg, honey, and sugar to the mug and beat with a fork until combined.

Add the almond flour, cinnamon, all-purpose flour, baking powder, and salt and beat again until smooth. Fold in half the berries and then top with the remainder.

To make the streusel, place all the ingredients in a small bowl and rub together with the tips of your fingers to bring together a bit like bread crumbs.

Spoon the streusel topping over the cake and cook in the microwave for 2 minutes 50 seconds @ 600W, 2 minutes 30 seconds @ 800W, or 2 minutes 10 seconds @ 1000W. Leave to cool slightly, then serve.

Tip

This is just as delicious without the streusel topping, so leave it out if you are running late! Or substitute frozen mixed berries. Just defrost slightly before usin

LEMON & POPPYSEED DRIZZLE

Make this cake for your grandma and she will be telling her friends about you and your baking skills for the rest of the year.

INGREDIENTS

2 tablespoons butter, softened

1 large egg

1 tablespoon lemon juice

½ teaspoon lemon extract

3 tablespoons superfine sugar

4 tablespoons all-purpose flour

¼ teaspoon baking powder

1 teaspoon poppyseeds

pinch of salt

To decorate

3 tablespoons confectioner's sugar

¼ teaspoon lemon extract

pinch of lemon zest

Swap the lemons
for oranges
or use both.

METHOD

Place the butter in a mug and microwave for 10–20 seconds until melted.

Add the egg, lemon juice, and lemon extract to the mug and beat with a fork until combined. Add the sugar, flour, baking powder, poppyseeds, and salt and beat again until smooth.

Grease or line a 1½ cup mug with plastic wrap, then pour in the cake batter.

Cook in the microwave for 2 minutes @ 600W, 1 minute 45 seconds @ 800W, or 1 minute 30 seconds @ 1000W. Turn the cake out onto a plate, remove the plastic wrap, and leave to cool.

Meanwhile, make the frosting. Mix together the confectioner's sugar and lemon extract, adding a drop of water to thin it if necessary. Spoon the frosting over the cake so that it trickles down the sides before it sets, then top with the lemon zest and serve.

BLACKBERRY CAKE

|||||||||||||||||||||||||||||||||||||||||||||||||||||||||||||||||||||||||||||||||||||||||||||||||||||||||||||||||||||

The blackberry, teamed with almond, is a force to be reckoned with. Raid the bushes when they're nice, plump, and juicy and stock up the freezer.

INGREDIENTS

2 tablespoons butter, softened

1 large egg

1 tablespoon 2% milk

1 teaspoon almond extract

3 tablespoons brown sugar

3 tablespoons almond flour

3 tablespoons all-purpose flour

¼ teaspoon baking powder

pinch of salt

2 tablespoons marzipan, diced

⅓ cup fresh blackberries

To decorate

½ teaspoon brown sugar

½ tablespoon sliced almonds

METHOD

Place the butter in a 1½ cup mug and microwave for 10–20 seconds until melted.

Add the egg, milk, almond extract, and sugar to the mug and beat with a fork until combined. Add the almond flour, all-purpose flour, baking powder, and salt and beat again until smooth. Fold in the marzipan and half the blackberries, then top with the remainder.

Cook in the microwave for 3 minute 35 seconds @ 600W, 3 minutes 15 seconds @ 800W or 2 minute 55 seconds @ 1000W. Leave to cool.

Sprinkle on the brown sugar and sliced almonds and serve.

Tip This is also delicious with the addition of 1 tablespoon grated apple.

HONEY CAKE

A little extra effort goes into this one, but when your best friend sees those little buzzy bees, you'll know it was all worth it.

INGREDIENTS

2 tablespoons butter, softened

1 large egg

2 tablespoons honey

½ teaspoon vanilla extract

3 tablespoons brown sugar

4 tablespoons all-purpose flour

¼ teaspoon baking powder

pinch of salt

To decorate

2 tablespoons butter, softened

4 tablespoons confectioner's sugar

pinch of cinnamon

1 tablespoon yellow marzipan

black food dye

4 sliced almonds

toothpick

Tip

Making the marzipan
bees a day in
advance means they
will firm up a little
and hold their shape.

METHOD

Place the butter in a 1½ cup mug and microwave for 10–20 seconds until melted.

Add the egg, honey, and vanilla to the mug and beat with a fork until combined. Add the sugar, flour, baking powder, and salt and beat again until smooth.

Cook in the microwave for 1 minute 45 seconds @ 600W, 1 minute 30 seconds @ 800W, or 1 minute 15 seconds @ 1000W. Leave to cool.

Meanwhile, make the frosting. Beat the butter, confectioner's sugar, and cinnamon together until light and fluffy, then spoon into a piping bag fitted with a large round nozzle.

Divide the marzipan in two and, with your fingers, roll each piece into two bumble bee-sized oval shapes. Dipping either a skewer or a paintbrush into the black food dye, paint the marzipan with stripes and eyes to look like a bee, finishing with almond slices for wings. Place one on a toothpick.

Once the cake is completely cool, pipe the frosting in a spiral pattern over the cake. It's best to work from the outside edge in and to keep constant pressure on the piping bag. To finish, release the pressure on the bag, press down lightly, and then pull straight up.

Garnish with the bees and drizzle with honey to serve.

RAINBOW CAKE

This colorful cake is the perfect pick-me-up so make it for anyone you notice is looking a little down. The rain clouds will clear and the sun will come out.

INGREDIENTS

2 tablespoons butter, softened

1 large egg

1 tablespoon 2% milk

1 teaspoon vanilla extract

3 tablespoons superfine sugar

4 tablespoons all-purpose flour

¼ teaspoon baking powder

pinch of salt

pink, yellow, green, blue food coloring

To decorate

1 tablespoon butter, softened

2 tablespoons confectioner's sugar

¼ teaspoon vanilla extract

1 rainbow marshmallow twist

Tip

Add the food coloring a little at a time as too much can ruin the taste. If using coloring pastes, use the end of a toothpick to scoop a little out.

METHOD

Place the butter in a 1½ cup mug and microwave for 10–20 seconds until melted.

Add the egg, milk, and vanilla to the mug and beat with a fork until combined. Add the sugar, flour, baking powder, and salt and beat again until smooth.

Divide the cake mixture among 4 small cups. Add a few drops of different food coloring to each pot and mix in well.

Spoon each of the colored cake mixtures into a 1½ cup mug and use a skewer or knife to swirl together the colors for a beautiful marbled effect.

Cook in the microwave for 2 minutes @ 600W, 1 minute 45 seconds @ 800W, or 1 minute 30 seconds @ 1000W. Leave to cool.

Meanwhile, make the frosting. Beat the butter, confectioner's sugar, and vanilla together until light and fluffy, then spoon into a piping bag fitted with a closed star nozzle. Pipe two 1-inch whirls.

Take a marshmallow twist candy, bend it, and stick each end into the frosting to create a lovely rainbow arch, then serve.

HALLOWEEN GHOST

This is so simple to make and decorate, it guarantees ghoulish fun for all ages.

INGREDIENTS

2 tablespoons butter, softened

2 ounces dark chocolate

1 large egg

2 tablespoons 2% milk

3 tablespoons superfine sugar

3 tablespoons all-purpose flour

¼ teaspoon baking powder

pinch of salt

For the chocolate ganache

4 tablespoons heavy cream

2 tablespoons dark chocolate, finely
chopped

To decorate

1 teaspoon confectioner's sugar

3–4 ounces white fondant icing

black food coloring

Make vanilla cake
(see recipe on page
38) and spread with
ganache or jam.

METHOD

First make the chocolate ganache. Place the cream in a mug and microwave for 20–30 seconds until nearly boiling. Add the chocolate and stir until melted and smooth. Set aside to cool a little and thicken. The longer you leave the ganache, the more it will set, so keep an eye on it to make sure you get a nice and thick but spreadable icing.

Grease a 1½ cup mug with a little butter and set aside. Place the remaining butter and chocolate into a second mug and microwave for 10–20 seconds until melted.

Add the egg and milk to the mug and beat together with a fork, then add the sugar, flour, baking powder, and salt and beat again until smooth. Transfer the cake mixture to the greased mug and cook in the microwave for 2 minutes 20 seconds @ 600W, 2 minutes @ 800W, or 1 minute 40 seconds @ 1000W. Turn the cake out onto a plate and leave to cool slightly.

Spread the ganache over the cooled cake. Dust a clean work surface with the confectioner's sugar and roll out the fondant to a size that will cover the entire cake. Cut a rough 6-inch round circle out of the fondant and gently lay this over the ganache-covered cake. Press down a little on top but leave the edges to fold slightly in waves.

Dip a paintbrush or toothpick in the black food coloring and draw on a face.

RED VELVET CAKE

IIIIIIIIIIIIIIIIIIIIIIIIIIIIIIIIIIIIIIIIIIIIIIIIIIIIIIIIIIIIIIIIIIIIIIIIIIIIIIIIIIIIIIIIIIIIIIIIIIIIIIIIIIIIIIIIIIIIIIIII

A card is boring, maybe flowers are too much, but a red velvet cake with cream cheese frosting is just right on Valentine's Day

INGREDIENTS

2 tablespoons butter, softened

1 large egg

1 teaspoon red food coloring

2 tablespoons buttermilk

1 teaspoon vanilla extract

3 tablespoons superfine sugar

3 tablespoons all-purpose flour

¼ teaspoon baking powder

1½ tablespoons cocoa powder

pinch of salt

¼ teaspoon white wine vinegar

To decorate

1 tablespoon butter, softened

1½ tablespoons cream cheese

3 tablespoons confectioner's sugar

¼ teaspoon red food coloring

METHOD

Place the butter in a 1½ cup mug and microwave for 10–20 seconds until melted.

Add the egg, red food coloring, buttermilk, and vanilla to the mug and beat with a fork until combined.

Add the sugar, flour, baking powder, cocoa, and salt, and beat again until smooth. Stir in the white wine vinegar.

Cook in the microwave for 2 minutes @ 600W, 1 minute 45 seconds @ 800W, or 1 minute 30 seconds @ 1000W. Leave to cool.

Meanwhile, make the frosting. Beat the butter, cream cheese, and confectioner's sugar together until smooth. Add the red food coloring one drop at a time, stirring after each addition until you achieve your desired shade of red, then spoon the frosting into a piping bag fitted with a closed star nozzle.

The effect you want from your frosting is that of a beautiful Valentine's rose so start in the center and, keeping steady pressure on the piping bag, move in a gradual spiral toward the outer edge, overlapping a little as you go. To finish, release pressure on the piping bag, press down slightly, and then pull away.

CHRISTMAS CAKE

Everyone loves a fruitcake for the holidays and the added appeal of this one is that you can make it in no time at all and without all the advance planning ... genius!

INGREDIENTS

1 tablespoon butter, softened, plus
 a little for greasing
1 tablespoon brandy
6 tablespoons mixed dried fruit
1 large egg
3 tablespoons brown sugar
$1/2$ teaspoon pumpkin pie spice
$1/2$ teaspoon cinnamon
1 teaspoon vanilla extract
1 tablespoon all -purpose flour
pinch of baking powder
pinch of salt
1 tablespoon candied cherries,
 halved
1 tablespoon candied mixed peel
2 tablespoons almonds, roughly
 chopped

To decorate
1 teaspoon confectioner's sugar
3 ounces ready-to-roll marzipan
1 tablespoon apricot jam
3 ounces fondant icing
3 tablespoons white frosting
$1/2$ teaspoon water
$1/2$ teaspoon white sprinkles
$1/4$ teaspoon edible gold stars

METHOD

Grease a $1^{1}/_2$ cup mug with a little butter and set aside. Place the butter, brandy, and dried fruit in a mug, and microwave for 10–20 seconds until melted. Add the egg, sugar, pumpkin pie spice, cinnamon, and vanilla and beat with a fork until combined. Add the flour, baking powder, salt, candied cherries, candied peel, and almonds and fold in.

Cook in the microwave for 3 minutes 20 seconds @ 600W, 3 minutes @ 800W, or 2 minute 40 seconds @ 1000W. Leave to cool until it comes away from the edges then turn out onto a plate to cool completely.

Dust a clean work surface with the confectioner's sugar and roll out the marzipan to a size large enough to cover the entire cake. Brush the cake with half the jam then lay over the marzipan, smoothing it down with your palm as you go, trimming any excess at the bottom with a sharp knife. Repeat the process with the fondant icing.

Mix the white frosting with the water to a thick consistency. Spoon over the center of the cake and allow to dribble down the sides. While still wet, scatter the sprinkles and gold stars.

Tip

Wrap in parchment paper and then colored tissue for a perfect homemade foodie gift.

PIÑA COLADA

This cake guarantees a little ray of sunshine on a cold winter's day.
Set up the lounge chair, break out the cocktail umbrellas, and enjoy!

INGREDIENTS

½ tablespoon dried coconut

1 large egg, yolk and white
separated

¼ cup finely chopped fresh
pineapple, plus a slice for garnish

2 tablespoons butter, softened

1 tablespoon white rum

3 tablespoons superfine sugar

2 tablespoons coconut milk

1 teaspoon vanilla extract

5 tablespoons all-purpose flour

¼ teaspoon baking powder

pinch of salt

To garnish

2 tablespoons heavy cream

½ tablespoon confectioner's sugar

1 tablespoon rum

1 pineapple leaf

1 candied cherry

½ tablespoon coconut flakes

1 cocktail umbrella

METHOD

Spread the coconut on a small plate. Take a 1½ cup mug and dip the rim first into the egg white and then into the coconut. Stick as much coconut as you can to the edge of the mug.

Add the pineapple, butter, rum, and superfine sugar to the mug and microwave for 1 minute until hot and bubbling. Leave to cool slightly.

Add the remaining egg white, egg yolk, coconut milk, and vanilla to the mug and beat with a fork until thoroughly combined. Add the flour, baking powder, and salt and beat again until smooth.

Cook in the microwave for 5 minutes 30 seconds @ 600W, 4 minutes 30 seconds @ 800W, or 3 minutes 30 seconds @ 1000W. Leave to cool.

Meanwhile, make the frosting. Beat together the cream, confectioner's sugar, and rum until light and fluffy, then spread over the cake, swirling with the back of a spoon. Garnish with the pineapple slice, pineapple leaf, cherry, and coconut, then add a big cocktail umbrella.

Tip

Make this non-alcoholic using pineapple juice in place of rum.

COKE FLOAT

||||||||||||||||||||||||||||||||||||||||||||||||||||||||||||||||||||||||||||||||||||||||||||||||||||||||||||||||||||||||||||||||||||||

Don't make the kids miss out on the happy hour fun—this old classic is just for them! Oh and, of course, all the big kids as well.

INGREDIENTS

2 tablespoons butter, softened

1 tablespoon cocoa powder

1 large egg

2 tablespoons cola

3 tablespoons superfine sugar

4 tablespoons all-purpose flour

$\frac{1}{4}$ teaspoon baking powder

pinch of salt

To decorate

$\frac{2}{3}$ tablespoon butter, softened

$\frac{1}{2}$ teaspoon cocoa powder

2 tablespoons confectioner's sugar

1 teaspoon cola

1 scoop vanilla ice cream

1 tablespoon cola gummy candies

METHOD

Place the butter in a 1 $\frac{1}{2}$ cup mug and microwave for 10–20 seconds until melted.

Add the cocoa and mix until well combined. Add the egg, cola, and sugar to the mug and beat together with a fork. Add the flour, baking powder, and salt and beat again until smooth.

Cook in the microwave for 2 minutes 20 seconds @ 600W, 2 minutes @ 800W, or 1 minute 40 seconds @ 1000W. Leave to cool.

Meanwhile, make the icing. Place the butter, cocoa powder, confectioner's sugar, and cola in a mug and stir together. Cook in the microwave for 10–15 seconds until melted, then stir again until smooth.

Top the cake with a scoop of ice cream and drizzle with the icing. Top with the cola bottles.

||||||||||||||||||||||||||||||||||||||||||||||||||||||||||||||

Go all out and make cherry cola floats! Use cherry cola in the cake and top with cherry ice cream.

MOCHA

When you're working late and you need something to keep going, this is just the thing—well, I'll make any excuse for some cake!

INGREDIENTS

1 tablespoon butter, softened

1 ounce dark chocolate, finely chopped

1 large egg

1 tablespoon 2% milk

2 teaspoons instant coffee, mixed with 1½ tablespoons hot water

2 tablespoons brown sugar

2 tablespoons all-purpose flour

⅛ teaspoon baking powder

pinch of salt

To decorate

1 tablespoon heavy cream

pinch of cocoa powder

1 teaspoon coffee beans

METHOD

Place the butter and chocolate in a small ¾ cup mug or teacup and microwave for 10–20 seconds until melted.

Add the egg, milk, and half the coffee to the mug and beat with a fork until thoroughly combined. Add the sugar, flour, baking powder, and salt and beat again until smooth.

Cook in the microwave for 2 minutes @ 600W, 1 minute 45 seconds @ 800W, or 1 minute 30 seconds @ 1000W.

Pierce the the cake all over with a toothpick and pour on the remaining coffee, then leave to cool slightly.

Top the cake with a thick swirl of cream, a dusting of cocoa, and one or two coffee beans.

Pouring the coffee over the cake keeps it moist and gives it a more intense coffee flavor than mixing it all in with the batter.

BAILEYS ON THE ROCKS

This one's a smooth-flavored Irish cream cake for grownups, with a few marshmallows for those days when you need extra indulgence.

INGREDIENTS

2 tablespoons butter, softened

½ teaspoon cocoa powder

1 large egg

2 tablespoons Baileys or other Irish cream liqueur

3 tablespoons superfine sugar

3 tablespoons all-purpose flour

¼ teaspoon baking powder

pinch of salt

To decorate

3 mini marshmallows

1 teaspoon Baileys

METHOD

Place the butter in a 1½ cup mug and microwave for 10–20 seconds until melted.

Add the cocoa to the mug and mix, then add the egg and Baileys and beat with a fork until thoroughly combined. Finally add the sugar, flour, baking powder, and salt, and beat again until smooth.

Cook in the microwave for 2 minutes @ 600W, 1 minute 45 seconds @ 800W, or 1 minute 30 seconds @ 1000W.

Top with the marshmallows and microwave for another 10–15 seconds until just melting. Drizzle on the Baileys and serve.

Tip

Why not try this topping on a brownie, a chocolate cake, or even melt it completely and drizzle over a sundae!

GUINNESS CAKE

||||||||||||||||||||||||||||||||||||||||||||||||||||||||||||||||||||||||||||||||||||||||||||||||||||||||||||||||

Dense and moist, this velvety Guinness cake makes a perfect thank you for Dad when he has agreed to pick you up from that late-night party.

INGREDIENTS

2 tablespoons butter, softened

1½ ounces dark chocolate, broken into pieces

1 large egg

3 tablespoons Guinness or other stout

3 tablespoons brown sugar

4 tablespoons all-purpose flour

¼ teaspoon baking powder

pinch of salt

To decorate

3 tablespoons confectioner's sugar

1½ tablespoons cream cheese

½ tablespoon white sprinkles

METHOD

Place the butter and chocolate in a 1½ cup mug and microwave for 10–20 seconds until melted.

Add the egg to the mug and beat with a fork until combined. Stir in the Guinness, then add the sugar, flour, baking powder, and salt and beat again until smooth.

Cook in the microwave for 2 minutes @ 600W, 1 minute 45 seconds @ 800W, or 1 minute 30 seconds @ 1000W. Leave to cool.

Meanwhile, make the frosting. Beat the confectioner's sugar and cream cheese together until smooth, then spread over the cooled cake, swirling with the back of a spoon. Scatter on the sprinkles to serve.

WHITE RUSSIAN

Make a statement with this amazing monochrome cocktail. The creamy marbled flavors work deliciously together and give this cocktail cake a real twist.

INGREDIENTS

2 tablespoons butter, softened

1 large egg

3 tablespoons superfine sugar

4 tablespoons all-purpose flour

¼ teaspoon baking powder

pinch of salt

1 tablespoon Kahlua or coffee liqueur

1 teaspoon cocoa powder

1 tablespoon vodka

1 teaspoon vanilla extract

To decorate

3 tablespoons heavy cream

1 tablespoon Kahlua

pinch cocoa powder

black and white striped straws

METHOD

Place the butter in a 1½ cup mug and microwave for 10–20 seconds until melted.

Add the egg and sugar and beat with a fork until combined, then add the flour, baking powder, and salt and beat again until smooth. Spoon half of the cake mixture into another mug or bowl and stir in the Kahlua and cocoa powder. Stir the vodka and vanilla into the other half.

Combine the two cake mixtures in one 1½ cup mug but do not mix—simply drag through a skewer or knife to creat a marbled effect. Cook in the microwave for 2 minutes 20 seconds @ 600W, 2 minutes @ 800W, or 1 minute 40 seconds @ 1000W. Leave to cool.

Meanwhile, make the frosting. Whip the heavy cream into soft peaks and then stir in the Kahlua. Spoon the frosting over the cake and sprinkle with the cocoa powder. Serve with little black and white straws.

 *Swap* Make this nonalcoholic by using coffee or melted chocolate in place of Kahlua, and milk instead of vodka.

MOJITO

A classic refreshing drink turned into a funky mug cake! This will remind you of your vacation and perhaps tempt you to book another.

INGREDIENTS

2 tablespoons butter, softened

1 large egg

1 tablespoon white rum

4 tablespoons superfine sugar

1 lime, zested

1 tablespoon lime juice

3 tablespoons all-purpose flour

¼ teaspoon baking powder

pinch of salt

To decorate

2 tablespoons butter, softened

4 tablespoons confectioner's sugar

¼ teaspoon peppermint essence

drop of green food coloring

1 slice of lime

1 teaspoon superfine sugar

3 mini marshmallows

1 toothpick

1 fresh mint sprig

Tip

This makes a great dessert and your friends will love the quirky presentation.

METHOD

Place the butter in a 1½ cup mug and microwave for 10–20 seconds until melted.

Add the egg, rum, sugar, lime zest, and juice to the mug and beat with a fork until combined. Add the flour, baking powder, and salt and beat again until smooth.

Cook in the microwave for 1 minute then another 1 minute 10 seconds @ 600W, 1 minute @ 800W, or 50 seconds @ 1000W. Leave to cool.

Meanwhile, make the frosting. Beat the butter, confectioner's sugar, and peppermint together until light and fluffy, then fold in the green coloring. Spoon into a piping bag fitted with a large closed star nozzle. Pipe the frosting over the cooled cake in a spiral pattern—it's best to work in from the outside edge, keeping constant pressure on the piping bag and working gradually toward the center. To finish, release the pressure on the bag, then press down lightly and pull straight up.

Dip the lime slice in a little water and then roll the edge through the sugar. Thread the marshmallows onto the toothpick and skewer into the top of the cake. Finish with the sugared lime and a mint sprig.

Treats

SALTED CARAMEL & CHOCOLATE

Salted caramel is ridiculously addictive. Here the salt sets off the caramel and dark chocolate perfectly.

INGREDIENTS

2 tablespoons butter, softened, plus a little for greasing

1½ ounces dark chocolate, finely chopped

1 large egg

1 tablespoon 2% milk

2 tablespoons brown sugar

3 tablespoons all-purpose flour

¼ teaspoon baking powder

2 tablespoons dulche de leche or thick caramel, mixed with ¼ teaspoon sea salt flakes

pinch of sea salt flakes

METHOD

Grease a 1½ cup mug with a little butter.

Place the remaining butter and chocolate in a second mug and microwave for 10–20 seconds until melted.

Add the egg and milk and beat with a fork until combined. Add the sugar, flour, and baking powder, and beat again until smooth, then transfer the mixture to the greased mug and spoon a tablespoon of the salty caramel on the top.

Cook in the microwave for 3 minutes 20 seconds @ 600W, 3 minutes @ 800W, or 2 minutes 40 seconds @ 1000W. Leave to cool.

Carefully turn the cake out onto a plate and spoon on the remaining caramel. Sprinkle with a few sea salt flakes and serve immediately.

Tip

Top with a scoop of vanilla, chocolate, or caramel ice cream.

LAMINGTONS

A traditional Australian treat! These little cakes are as fun and messy to make as they are to eat!

INGREDIENTS

2 tablespoons butter, softened, plus
  a little to grease
1 large egg
1 tablespoon 2% milk
2 teaspoons vanilla extract
3 tablespoons superfine sugar
4 tablespoons all-purpose flour
$\frac{1}{4}$ teaspoon baking powder
pinch of salt

To decorate

2 tablespoons butter, softened
1 teaspoon cocoa powder
3 tablespoons confectioner's sugar
3 tablespoons dried coconut
3 tablespoons heavy cream
1 tablespoon strawberry jam

Tip

Purists wouldn't slice
the cake and serve
with cream and jam
so leave it out if
you wish.

METHOD

Grease a 1$\frac{1}{2}$ cup mug with a little butter and set aside. Place the butter in a second mug and microwave for 10–20 seconds until melted.

Add the egg, milk, and vanilla to the mug and beat with a fork until combined. Add the sugar, flour, baking powder, and salt and beat again until smooth.

Cook in the microwave for 2 minutes 20 seconds @ 600W, 2 minutes @ 800W, or 1 minute 40 seconds @ 1000W. Leave to cool.

Meanwhile, make the frosting. Place the butter, cocoa, and confectioner's sugar in a mug and microwave for 10–15 seconds until melted. Stir to combine.

Scatter the coconut evenly on a plate. Turn the cooled cake out of the mug and then dip the entire cake in the chocolate frosting. Immediately transfer the chocolate-coated cake to the plate and roll so the coconut is distributed evenly over the surface. Leave for a few minutes while you wait for the frosting to set.

Meanwhile, whip the cream into soft peaks. Slice the cake in half horizontally and spread the top of the bottom piece with the jam. Add a spoonful of whipped cream and then place the other piece of cake on top.

RASPBERRY & PISTACHIO RICE CRISPIES

Okay, so you might argue that this is not strictly a cake, and I would insist that it is (it's a crispy cake), but whichever side of the fence you're on, I am sure we will both agree that it's one of the tastiest things that has ever come out of a microwave.

INGREDIENTS

4 tablespoons marshmallow fluff or mini marshmallows
6 tablespoons Rice Crispies
1 tablespoon dark chocolate chunks
1 tablespoon dried raspberries
1 tablespoon pistachios, roughly chopped

METHOD

Place the marshmallow fluff in a 1½ cup mug and microwave for 10–15 seconds until melted.

Fold in the Rice Crispies, chocolate chunks, raspberries, and pistachios.

Cook in the microwave for 12 seconds @ 600W, 10 seconds @ 800W, or 8 seconds @ 1000W.

Serve warm and gooey or leave to set and enjoy like a crispy cake.

Tip

If you like your crispy cake to be slightly chewy, line your mug with plastic wrap before you start. Once cooked, turn it out onto a plate, remove the plastic wrap, and leave to cool.

CHOCOLATE, GINGER & PEAR CAKE

If you ever need a fancy dessert in a hurry—this is it. It's simple to whip up and sophisticated enough for the classiest soirée.

INGREDIENTS

1 tablespoon butter, softened
1 ounce dark chocolate, finely
  chopped
½ large egg, lightly beaten
1 tablespoon 2% milk
2 tablespoons superfine sugar
2 tablespoons all-purpose flour
1/8 teaspoon baking powder
¼ teaspoon ground ginger
pinch of salt
1 tablespoon finely chopped
  candied ginger in syrup
1 ripe pear, peeled

To decorate
1 tablespoon candied ginger syrup
pinch of cocoa powder

METHOD

Place the butter and chocolate in a 1½ cup mug and microwave for 10–20 seconds until melted.

Add the egg and milk to the mug and beat with a fork until combined.

Add the sugar, flour, baking powder, ground ginger, and salt and beat again until smooth. Fold through the chopped ginger. Slice off the base of the pear so it will sit up in the mug and then press down into the mixture.

Cook in the microwave for 2 minutes 10 seconds @ 600W, 1 minute 50 seconds @ 800W, or 1 minute 30 seconds @ 1000W. Leave to cool.

Drizzle with a little ginger syrup and dust with cocoa powder, then serve.

Swap

Swap the dark chocolate for white and add ½ teaspoon vanilla extract.

CHOCOLATE CHIP COOKIE

Once again I have snuck in a recipe that isn't really a cake, but variety is the spice of life, and you'll want this instant cookie recipe in your microwave repertoire … trust me.

INGREDIENTS

1 tablespoon butter, softened
1 tablespoon superfine sugar
1 tablespoon brown sugar
1 large egg yolk
¼ teaspoon vanilla extract
3 tablespoons all-purpose flour
pinch of salt
2 tablespoons chocolate chips

METHOD

Place the butter in a large ramekin or small mug and microwave for 10–20 seconds until melted.

Add the superfine sugar, brown sugar, and egg yolk, and beat together with a fork. Add the vanilla, flour, and salt, and beat again until combined, then fold in the chocolate chips (leaving a few at the top, which will become gooey). Flatten the dough with the back of a spoon.

Cook in the microwave for 1 minute 10 seconds @ 600W, 1 minute @ 800W, or 50 seconds @ 1000W. Leave to stand for 10 minutes.

Tip If you leave this cookie to stand for 10 minutes, it will still be warm but also deliciously chewy.

STICKY TOFFEE

If someone catches you eating this mug of pure bliss and suggests that you might like to share with them, next time be sure to lock the kitchen door.

INGREDIENTS

2 tablespoons butter, softened plus
  a little for greasing
4 tablespoons caramel sauce
1 large egg
1 teaspoon vanilla extract
2 tablespoons dried dates, roughly
  chopped
3 tablespoons brown sugar
4 tablespoons all-purpose flour
¼ teaspoon baking powder
pinch of ground cloves
pinch of salt

METHOD

Grease a 1½ cup mug with a little butter and then spoon in 3 tablespoons of the caramel sauce.

Place the butter in a second mug and microwave for 10–20 seconds until melted.

Add the egg, a tablespoon of caramel sauce, the vanilla, and dried dates and beat together with a fork.

Fold in the sugar, flour, baking powder, ground cloves, and salt, and beat again until smooth. Spoon this cake mixture into the mug with the caramel sauce.

Cook in the microwave for 2 minutes 35 seconds @ 600W, 2 minutes 15 seconds @ 800W, or 1 minute 55 seconds @ 1000W. Leave to cool.

Carefully turn the cake out onto a plate, ensuring you scrape all the toffee goodness from the bottom of the mug and none goes to waste! Serve immediately with a scoop of ice cream if you wish.

Tip

Mix a tablespoon of cocoa powder in with the flour to bring a little chocolate flavor to the party.

ROCKY ROAD

Rocky road is the stuff that dreams are made of, so get in the kitchen and make yours come utterly, deliciously true!

INGREDIENTS

2 tablespoons butter, softened
1 tablespoon cocoa powder
1 large egg
3 tablespoons superfine sugar
2 tablespoons all-purpose flour
$^1/_3$ teaspoon baking powder
pinch of salt
4 tablespoons mini marshmallows
2 tablespoons raisins
2 tablespoons graham
   cracker pieces

METHOD

Place the butter in a 1½ cup mug and microwave for 10–20 seconds until melted.

Stir in the cocoa powder until combined, then add the egg and sugar and beat with a fork until combined.

Add the flour, baking powder, and salt and beat again until smooth. Fold in almost all the marshmallows, raisins, and graham cracker pieces, and then top with the remaining.

Cook in the microwave for 2 minutes 20 seconds @ 600W, 2 minutes @ 800W, or 1 minute 40 seconds @ 1000W. Leave to cool slightly before munching away.

Tip

There are so many possible variations with this cake, so have fun adding nuts, using different dried fruit, and trying different cookies, like chocolate chip cookies.

CHOCOLATE FUDGE S'MORES

S'mores, a traditional campfire treat, inspired this little mug cake recipe and provided the perfect excuse to eat lots of marshmallows.

INGREDIENTS

2 tablespoons butter, softened

2 tablespoons cocoa

1 large egg

2 tablespoons 2% milk

3 tablespoons superfine sugar

3 tablespoons all-purpose flour

¼ teaspoon baking powder

pinch of salt

2 crushed graham crackers

2 tablespoons marshmallow fluff or mini marshmallows

METHOD

Place the butter in a mug and microwave for 10–20 seconds until melted.

Stir in the cocoa until combined, then add the egg and milk and beat with a fork until combined. Add the sugar, flour, baking powder, and salt and beat again until smooth.

Press the crushed graham crackers into the bottom of a 1½ cup mug. Spoon in the cake mixture and top with the marshmallow.

Cook in the microwave for 2 minutes @ 600W, 1 minute 45 seconds @ 800W or 2 minutes 30 seconds @ 1000W. Serve immediately.

As a nod to the classic S'mores, place the mug under the broiler for 30 seconds until the marshmallow is nicely caramelized and chewy. Just make sure you use a sturdy mug!

CHOCOLATE & CARAMEL POPCORN SUNDAE

///

Make this cake when you're in the mood for a movie night treat. Pile it high with ice cream, popcorn, and delicious sweet sauce. Don't forget a saucer to catch the drips!

INGREDIENTS

2 tablespoons butter, softened
1½ ounces dark chocolate, finely chopped
1 large egg
2 tablespoons 2% milk
3 tablespoons superfine sugar
3 tablespoons all-purpose flour
¼ teaspoon baking powder
pinch of salt

To decorate
1 scoop vanilla ice cream
a handful of caramel popcorn
1 tablespoon caramel sauce
1 tablespoon chocolate sauce

METHOD

Place the butter and chocolate in a 1¼ cup sundae bowl and microwave for 10–20 seconds until melted.

Add the egg and milk to the glass and beat with a fork until combined. Add the sugar, flour, baking powder, and salt and beat again until smooth.

Cook in the microwave for 2 minutes 20 seconds @ 600W, 2 minutes @ 800W, or 1 minute 40 seconds @ 1000W. Leave to cool slightly.

Top with a scoop of ice cream, sprinkle on the caramel popcorn, and finish with a generous drizzle of both sauces.

UPSIDE-DOWN APPLE & CINNAMON CAKE

This sticky upside-down cake can be made with a variety of fruits but here I marry up a classic pair—apple and cinnamon—with a little caramel sauce.

INGREDIENTS

2 tablespoons butter, softened, plus
  a little for greasing
3 thin slices of red-skinned apple
1 large egg
1 tablespoon 2% milk
1 teaspoon vanilla extract
3 tablespoons brown sugar
4 tablespoons all-purpose flour
1/4 teaspoon baking powder
1 teaspoon cinnamon
pinch of salt
3 tablespoons grated apple

To decorate

1 tablespoon caramel sauce
1/4 teaspoon brown sugar
ice cream, optional

METHOD

Grease a 1 1/2 cup mug with a little butter, then fan out the apple slices and place at the bottom.

Place the remaining butter in a second mug and microwave for 10–20 seconds until melted.

Add the egg, milk, and vanilla to the melted butter and beat with a fork until combined.

Add the sugar, flour, baking powder, cinnamon, and salt, and beat again until smooth. Fold in the grated apple then gently pour the mixture over the sliced apple.

Cook in the microwave for 2 minutes 20 seconds @ 600W, 2 minutes @ 800W or 1 minute 40 seconds @ 1000W. Leave to cool slightly.

Carefully turn the cake out onto a plate. Drizzle with caramel sauce and sprinkle on some brown sugar to serve, and add a scoop of ice cream if you like.

LEMON CURD CHEESECAKE

Instant cheesecake ... a great invention, but also slightly dangerous! Don't forget to chill this one properly before eating it, so it tastes its best.

INGREDIENTS

½ tablespoon butter, softened

2 tablespoons crushed graham crackers

1 large egg

3 tablespoons cream cheese

2 tablespoons sour cream

¼ teaspoon vanilla extract

3 tablespoons superfine sugar

¼ teaspoon cornstarch

pinch of salt

To decorate

2 tablespoons lemon curd

1 long piece of curled lemon zest

METHOD

Place the butter in a 1¼ cup jar or mug and microwave for 10–20 seconds until melted. Stir in the graham-cracker crumbs and then press down with the back of a spoon to create a crust at the bottom of the mug.

In a separate mug add the egg, cream cheese, sour cream, vanilla, superfine sugar, cornstarch, and salt. Beat together with a fork until smooth and combined and then spoon the mixture over the graham-cracker crust.

Cook in the microwave in 30 second bursts with 20 second breaks in between for 2 minutes @ 600W, 1 minute 45 seconds @ 800W, or 1 minute 30 seconds @ 1000W.

Chill in the fridge for at least 1 hour before topping with the lemon curd and lemon zest curl.

Tip

Sometimes it's a good idea to break up the cooking time so that the mixture doesn't overheat and explode! That's the reasoning behind cooking this one in a few short bursts.

INDEX

THANK YOUS

Where to start, what a whirlwind! This book has come together in such a short period. It is incredible what you can accomplish with an amazing team. The recent and instant interest in mug cakes put the wheels in motion at a speed we were not expecting. So thank you to everyone at Kyle Books who helped to shape the book into what you see now. It really was a great team effort.

To Judith and Kyle, thank you for believing in me and giving me the chance to get *Mug Cakes* out there and into people's microwaves! What a fun and exciting subject for my cookbook debut. To Claire, thank you for all your great support behind the scenes.

The lovely Vicki, you made me laugh throughout. Your support and advice was invaluable. I hope your new microwave has you "mug caking," as well as warming up milk for your new arrival. And once again to Judith, who took over seamlessly; you are always a step ahead, and it's a delight to work with you.

Olivia and Wei, thank you both for searching high and low for the perfect mugs and for all the fun, quirky knick-knacks in between. Nicky, thank you for bringing your wonderful style to *Mug Cakes*. It brings all our hard work together perfectly.

To Tara, who took on the challenge of bringing *Mug Cakes* to life; no one could have more enthusiasm for mugs, cakes, and crazy toppings than you. Thank you for being excited about each and every mug cake I put in front of you and your camera.

And finally to Tom, for being utterly disappointed if there wasn't a cake to taste, for your MasterChef style critiques, your endless support and for "food styling" my dinner when all I had eaten all day was cake. Your enthusiasm could not have been heightened, even if it was your own book. You are truly wonderful.

THANK YOUS

95